G. Barsali - U. Castelli - R. Gagetti - O .Parra

History and Masterpieces

of

PISA

New Edition

BONECHI EDIZIONI "IL TURISMO" FIRENZE

The articles on the Museo dell'Opera del Duomo and the Museo delle Sinopie were written by: **Antonio Chinca**

Photos: Bonechi Archives; Paolo Bacherini
Layout: Barbara Bonechi
Cover: Claudia Baggiani
Reprohouse: La Fotolitografia, Florence

ISBN 88-7204-188-0

Piazza del Duomo seen from the Porta di Santa Maria.

PISA IN HISTORY

Only scattered and fragmentary bits of information regarding Pisa's origins have come down to us, since the " historical facts " recorded by Pliny and Strabo are largely based on legend.

Therefore, the city's origins will continue to be shrouded in the same mystery that not even the great historians of long ago were able to solve. However, the original inhabitants of Pisa might well have been seamen who settled in the area of what is now the Medieval city during the pre-Roman period. It matters little whether they were Phoenicians or Greeks, since no record of their wandering has come down to us, but then neither did the Etruscans manage to leave us any trace of their civilization. Roman Pisa, on the other hand, is not at all mysterious. A colony was founded following a victory won by an allied force of Roman and Pisan troops over the Ligurians. The Emperor Augustus then increased the strength of the colony which, in the meantime, had become a flourishing sea-

port. In the year 180 A. D. the city requested and was granted the privilege of coming under Latin law. The history of the city thereafter gets lost inside the mainstream of Roman history in general.

In 476 A. D. barbarian tribes swooped down into Italy and Rome, in decline, never recovered. Goths and Byzantines took over the rule of the Italian peninsula including Pisa. Later, in the 7th century Pope Gregory the Great received aid from the Pisan navy in an expedition against the Byzantines.

The Longobards conquered all of Tuscany. Actually, no blood was spilled; it would be better to speak of a peaceful blending of the native Tuscan element with the Longobard strain. During the time of Charlemagne and his Carolingians, the city enjoyed relative independence.

But it was not until the 10th century A. D. that Pisa really began to experience her fabulous age of glory and extraordinary economic prosperity. The city looked to the sea, for her fortune lay in her navy. She fought bravely against the Saracens from Sicily, conquering Reggio Calabria in 1017 and then managed to drive her former allies out of Sardinia. This clash between Pisa and Genoa might easily have been the original cause of the rivalry which grew up between the two powerful maritime republics.

Conquest after conquest followed: Carthage, Bona and Lipari fell to Pisan land and sea troops during the years from 1030 to 1035. Jacopo Ciurini led the conquest of Corsica and the final subjection of Sardinia to Pisa, whereby the Pisan state was greatly enlarged (1051-1052).

In 1099, the Pisans flocked in large numbers to join the first crusade. In the 12th century they established trading bases along the Syrian coast. The Roman Emperor of the East, Alexius Comnenus, granted the Pisan merchants special landing privileges at Constantinople as well as the right to reductions in the duties to be paid.

Between 1114-1116 the Balearic Islands with Ibiza, Majorca, and Minorca fell to the Pisans. Archbishop Pietro Moriconi led the Pisan navy to victory in the name of the Cross, but clearly in the name of the Pisan state's political interests as well.

As a result of this and other exploits, the free city of Italy became a respected and feared power. This was the period when Pisa became the meeting place of two civilizations, the East and the West—taking on, in fact, the leadership of the latter. During the fierce struggles between the Papacy (Guelphs) and the Emperor (Ghibellines), Pisa was quick to side with the emperors, the greatest of whom, Frederick II, was particularly fond of the city. In 1241 Pisa was excommunicated for having kidnapped the bishops and cardinals who were on their way to a council meeting with the pope. The Ghibelline party soon succeeded in dominating the Guelphs.

In 1250 Frederick died. The other Tuscan cities, in particular Florence and Lucca, joined in an alliance against Pisa who was compelled to pay dearly for her defeat. Then on August 6, 1284 the Pisan and Genoese armadas clashed in the vicinity of the Isle of Meloria, not far from the mouth of the Arno River, and the Pisans took a terrible beating. The main cause for the defeat was attributed to the betrayal of a Pisan nobleman, Ugolino della Gherardesca, and when the political situation worsened even more, he was seized and locked up inside the Gualandi Tower together with his children and nephews.

Towards the end of the 13th century, ominous signs of political decline cropped up in the city and serious internal disputes poisoned its political life. In 1311 Henry VII of Luxembourg swept down through Italy to restore his party to its former glory. Ghibelline Italy flocked to join the cause of the young Germanic emperor, and Pisa followed suit. But then two years later, in circumstances not entirely clear, the emperor fell dead near Siena. His remains were laid to rest in Tino di Camaino's sarcophagus in the Cathedral.

When the Guelphs managed to seize power, the liberty which had been enjoyed by Ghibelline Pisa, as well as her independent and democratic spirit, was lost. The first despot to rule over the city, Uguccione della Faggiola, was partially successful in restoring the Pisan state to its former glory when he taught the citizens of Lucca a cruel lesson by conquering their city in 1315. But Uguccione was too much of a tyrant and for this reason he was ousted in 1316.

Other despots then rose to power: the Gherardescas, the Gambacortis, and Giovanni dell'Agnello, whose rule left horrible memories. In 1392 Pisa was sold to the Viscontis from Milan who in turn ceded it to the Florentines for a considerable sum. At this point, the flame of liberty was violently reignited and a revolt against Florence spontaneously broke out. But in 1406, after being subjected to a terrible siege, Pisa was forced to surrender to avoid starvation. In 1499 the Florentine troops once more succeeded in crushing their brave yet unlucky enemies. Thus, the ancient republic, the free city state, and all the liberties so dear to the people of Pisa fell before the reality of the new times.

Pisa under Florentine domination was ruled by the Medicis up until 1737, the year in which the last of the Medicis, Gastone, died without leaving an heir. The Grand Dukes of Lorraine, a minor branch of the Hapsburg line, succeeded the Medici dynasty. Even today the Lorraine rule is recognized as having been positive for the whole grand duchy of Tuscany, and Pisa was no exception. But, nevertheless, life had been drained out of the city and in 1860 after the bloodless Tuscan revolution Pisa meekly joined the new Italian state.

Today Pisa is a mediumsized provincial town with a population of 110,000, 20,000 of whom are university students. Even though the sea has receded several miles, it is still the focal point of all Pisan life. The reason lies in Pisa's history which, like the sea itself, is impermeated with the taste of salt water.

Opposite page: *the Leaning Tower and the apse of the cathedral.*

Pisa in Art History

Although the Phoenicians, Greeks, and Etruscans left no trace in Pisa, the Romans adorned the city with splendid buildings and public baths. Numerous Roman sarcophagi preserved in the Camposanto (monumental cemetery) are proof of the city' s classical heritage. In addition, huge quantities of building materials were unearthed in the Roman ruins and reutilized in the construction of the Cathedral and other monuments in the city such as the Baptistry and the Leaning Tower. These stones are still visible today—on a number of them you can read Latin inscriptions in memory of Hadrian and Trajan. As far back as the 8th century, Pisa stood out as a minor cultural center; in fact, the grammatician Pietro of Pisa was summoned to Paris by Charlemagne who, more illiterate than not, wanted to employ Pietro as his teacher. But it was not until the 11th century that the city's extraordinary artistic prospects began to open up: in 1063 Buscheto Pisano began work on the Cathedral, the first monument to be built out of the four that make up

the city's architectural heart. Buscheto became the most masterful interpreter of the Pisan Romanesque style which was born from the harmonious fusion of Oriental architectural and decorative motifs with Western architectural elements. This could very well have been the first time that East and West met harmoniously in the Pisan churches . Pointed arches, polychrome decorations, dark and light alternating stripes, pilaster strips, and lozenge patterns are echoes reverberating in Pisan Romanesque of the great sea eastward voyages. In Apulia, Sardinia Corsica, Lucca, Pistoia, and Siena, churches and bell towers were designed and put up in the style so dear to Buscheto, Diotisalvi, and Bonanno Pisano. Even the cathedral of the far away city of Split in Yugoslavia was built in the Pisan Romanesque style. Between 1063 and 1173 the Cathedral, the Baptistry, and the famous Leaning Tower were all begun. The Gothic monumental cemetery (where one day the young composer Franz Liszt would be inspired to write

Piazza dei Miracoli with the Baptistry in the foreground.

Sculptures by Nicola and Giovanni Pisano (Museo dell' Opera del Duomo).

his immortal " Totentanz ") was started in 1278 by Giovanni di Simone who also worked on the Leaning Tower after Bonanno Pisano's death.

Pisan painting comes into its own right on a national scale with the unknown " Master of San Martino", whose work slightly antedates Cimabue and Duccio di Buoninsegna—and who, in fact, may be considered the latter's rightful master. Another 13th century artist, Giunta Pisano, was the first Western painter to break away from the severe Byzantine tradition by rendering his Christ on the Cross both human and suffering. But it is in sculpture that the Pisans capture truly universal acclaim through two great artists whose very names stand for 13th century Italian sculpture: Nicola and Giovanni Pisano. They found, as nobody before them had been able to, motifs of great expressive liberty in the city's political condition and atmosphere.

Nicola Pisano, before anyone else, focused his attention on the classical heritage of his city and country. And, before any other Italian sculptor, he succeeded in conveying the classical fascination of antique statues. Thus, his Virgins look like Greek goddesses and his saints and prophets resemble aristocratic Romans. An outstanding example is the small nude figure just beneath the Adoration of the Magi scene on the Baptistry pulpit. Whether or not Nicola's main purpose was an anatomical study of the human body, we still may consider this figure very advanced for its times. Nicola's son, Giovanni, was not to be outdone by his father as can be seen in his rendering of the Hercules figure on the Cathedral pulpit. Both artists were probably cause for discussions and arguments, yet they were free to work as they pleased since they lived in a city which was basically democratic and independent. The sculptors joined their single talents together to produce one of Italy's loveliest fountains (in Perugia), whereby creating a great masterpiece. Giovanni Pisano was the greatest example of the drama, the torment, and the human tragedy of his century, the century whose poetic expression came from Dante Alighieri and whose pictorial genius was embodied in Giotto di Bondone. Giovanni Pisano's art forged generation upon generation of great sculptors and opened the way to the Renaissance splendors of Jacopo della Quercia, Ghiberti, Donatello, and Michelangelo.

THE LEANING TOWER

Few monuments in the whole world are as famous as this one. Its amazing inclination measures approximately 15 feet. Bonanno Pisano and Guglielmo started work on the tower in 1173, even though the date given in the Latin inscription to the right of the entrance is 1174 (actually, this date refers to the Pisan calendar set one year ahead). Some months after work was begun, the tower's first level was completed. Around this lower level there are columns set into the wall with classical capitals and blind arches with lozenge designs. Work continued under the direction of Bonanno who, in addition, sculpted the four bronze doors of the Cathedral in 1180, only one of which survived the disastrous 1595 fire. In 1185 the tower, having been built up to the third floor, already began to take on the architectural appearance it has today. At this point, owing to the crumbly state of the ground upon which Pisa stands, the first subsiding of the construction took place. In fact, a good number of buildings, some put up before and others after the Leaning Tower, lean over just like the famous tower in Pisa. Therefore, we had better set the record straight right off: the Leaning Tower of Pisa was never vertical and its tilt was noted immediately during construction. Bonanno left Pisa that year, in 1185 to go south to Sicily where a year later he sculpted another bronze door, this time for the Cathedral of Monreale. He came back to his native city only to find death awaiting him and was given honorable burial in a sarcophagus placed at the foot of his tower (it was discovered in 1820). The fact that he never saw his famous tower completed was probably a great disappointment to Bonanno. Later, in 1198, a number of bells were temporarily set up on the still

The Leaning Tower.
Opposite page: ***cross section of the Belltower.***

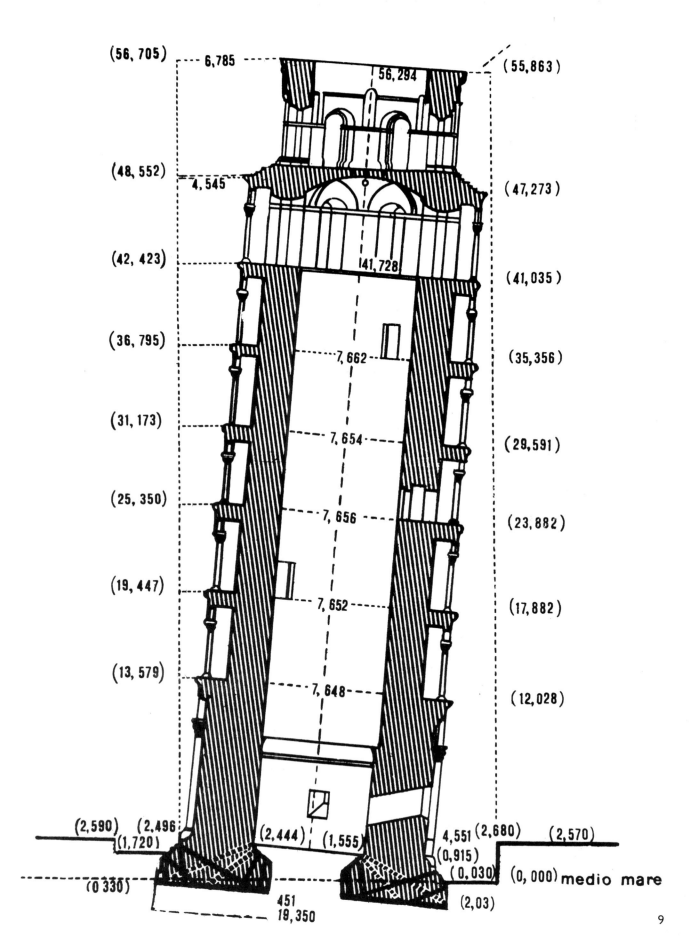

9

unfinished building. During the first half of the 13th century, serious political disorders prevented the completion of the work, as the wars against Genoa, Florence, and Lucca absorbed the best part of the city's energies; defending their liberty and independence was uppermost in the Pisans' minds. Work was picked up again in 1275 by Giovanni di Simone, the great architect responsible for the Church of St. Francis and the Camposanto Monumental Cemetery. It was interrupted once again in 1284, the year the Pisans suffered their great naval defeat at the hands of the Genoese. By 1319 the Leaning Tower was built up to the belfry. The belfry itself was added on in the years immediately following 1350 by Tommaso Pisano who with delicate skill managed to blend in the Gothic elements of the monument's upper tier with the predominantly Romanesque ones of the tower.

The exterior walls are about 14 feet across at the base and about 7 at the top. The tower is 179 feet tall and every year its inclination increases. The problem of the Leaning Tower has now burst forth in full and measures are being taken to correct it and save the Tower. The Leaning Tower is one of the many typically Italian bell towers although several art historians maintain that the origins of the Italian bell tower go back to the Muslim minaret. Just as the Muezzin sing out their calls to prayer from the minaret, the voice of the tolling bells summons the Christian believers for the same purpose. Other experts claim it was just the opposite, and that it could have been the Arabs who were influenced by the bell towers of the Christian churches so common in prelslamic Syria. Leaving aside these scholarly controversies, it is safe to say that the Leaning Tower of Pisa is well known and loved throughout the entire world. Perhaps the Italians are just a bit fonder of it than anyone else, since for them the tower stands for something special; it has become a symbol of their beloved homeland.

The Leaning Tower.

THE CATHEDRAL

The façade of the Cathedral is the work of Rainaldo, Buscheto's last successor, who was active during the second half of the 13th century. In the upper righthand section of the central portal, a Latin inscription reading " Rainaldus prudens operator.... " may be clearly made out. Just as in most of the Pisan churches, the façade faces westwards as if in respect for the glory that was once Western civilization. The mosaics in the lunette were designed by Alessio Baldovinetti in 1467 and later restored in 1829. The mosaic in the middle depicts the Assumption of the Virgin, the one on the left St. Reparata, and the one on the right St. John the Baptist. Two superb classical columns flank the central portal, while arches, lozenge designs, and rosettes of Oriental inspiration are used in profusion all over the lower section of the façade. The upper part of the façade makes use of Lombard arcading which is repeated as the major architectural motif in the Leaning Tower and on the Cathedral's main apse. The eye sweeps up a sequence of four rows of arcades which create an impressive perspective of arches and colonnades, just as harmonious and impressive as musical counterpoints.

In the upper righthand section of the second gallery there is a small Oriental red porphyry columnette which was carried from Majorca to Pisa. According to a charming old legend whoever looks at it is safe from betrayals in love for a day.

Inside the last arch on the left side of the Cathedral façade, the Pisans of long ago decided it would be the right place to give Buscheto honorable burial. In fact, the great architect who designed the Pisa Cathedral was laid to rest in a Roman sarcophagus because it was Rome and her temples which had influenced him when he was working on the imposing church. The epitaph inscribed along the top of the sarcophagus consecrates the glory of the great architect throughout eternity.

The cathedral: transept and apse.

Following page: *the cathedral and the Leaning Tower.*

The inscription on the Tomb of Buscheto on the cathedral facade. Below: *Virgin and child, the Evangelists and the Angels, the statues at the top of the façade.*

Opposite page: *the cathedral façade.*

The lunette over the central door with the Madonna by Giuseppe di Modena da Lucca; left: *detail of the capitals.*
Facing page: *the central door.*

The Central Doorway of the Cathedral

The original doors which Bonanno Pisano created in 1180 were destroyed in a terrible fire which broke out in 1595. Later the Florentine architect, Raphael Pagni, was commissioned by Grand Duke Ferdinand I to design three new ones. A group of Florentine sculptors, possibly students of Giambologna, carried out Pagni's design. The panels on the central door depict the life of the Virgin, while those on the side doors portray the life of Christ. Actually, the new doors are a far cry from the stylistic perfection of Ghiberti's " Door of Paradise" on the Florentine Baptistry. And they are equally far from Bonanno Pisano's severe and extremely concise style. Each panel is noteworthy for its fine perspective and its border decoration, in truth a bit heavy-handed, which is typical of the Baroque style then the dominant note in Italian art. On the lefthand side of the central door corresponding to the Nativity of the Virgin panel, a number of brilliant figures may be picked out, e.g. the dog, the frog, and two tiny lizards. Legend would have in that you can make your dreams come true by touching them.

Lunette of the side portal, with St. John the Baptist by Giuseppe di Modena da Lucca; below: *detail of the bronze panels from the central door.*

The St. Ranieri Door

When Bonanno Pisano was forced to abandon work on the Leaning Tower, he turned his attention to sculpting the set of four wonderful portals for the Cathedral. The three façade doors were completely destroyed in the 1595 fire, whereas the fourth, named for St. Ranieri since it opens into the chapel dedicated to the saint, survived and is still in excellent condition today. The work is of great artistic value and even though it lacks that finished perfection, it is nevertheless full of poetry and purity. Byzantine influence is strongly felt in the severe, ascetic-looking figures set into each panel. But in the Nativity, Flight into Egypt, and Crucifixion scenes, it is easy to pick out the humanity, poetic sense, and drama foreshadowing the realistic feeling which characterizes the second period of Italian Medieval sculpture.

Right: *The St. Ranieri door by Bonanno Pisano;* below: *the St. Ranieri door where the central nave meets with the transept.*

Three panels from the St. Ranieri door with Scenes from the Life of Christ by Bonanno Pisano.

Opposite page: *detail of the lozenge decorations on the apse of the cathedral.*

The Interior of the Cathedral

The Cathedral, the first of the four monuments in Piazza dei Miracoli, was begun in 1063. It probably went up on the site where the Emperor Hadrian's palace and later the Church of Santa Reparata once stood. The Cathedral was consecrated by Pope Gelasius II in 1118. Buscheto was the first of the Cathedral's architects. A Pisan, he had previously worked in Rome. During the second half of the 13th century work was picked up again and terminated by Rainaldo who worked on the front of the church and the stupendous façade. The building was completed approximately two centuries after it had been started. The Cathedral of Pisa, a superb and grandiose double-aisled church, has come down to us as one of the most beautiful in all Christendom. Its great size was most unusual for its time, and may be considered a living symbol of the Pisans' great religious fervor and the economic power of their republic.

Romanesque civilization in Italy triumphed and became identified with the Cathedral of Pisa. The full, rounded Romanesque arches and the slender, harmonious gallery of evident Lombard influence, blend in an unsurpassable harmony of lines, marbles, and colors, with pilaster strips and lozenge designs, and with pointed, Islamic-inspired arches and the polychrome decoration of alternating black and white bands.

The Cathedral is one of the rare Italian churches with double aisles like the basilicas of ancient Rome. However, the huge basilica shape of the church is crossed sideways by a new element, i.e., the transept, which creates the shape of a Latin cross. The imposing granite columns supporting the arcade were carried off from Palermo as spoils of war. They come from Palermo's most important mosque destroyed by the militia of the Pisan Maritime Republic in 1063.

The carved wooden ceiling replaces the original one which was destroyed in the 1595 fire. It is certainly an outstanding piece of work, but it clashes too much with the simple, stately lines of the Pisan Romanesque style.

The painting inside the dome depicting the Assumption of the Virgin is by Orazio Riminaldi. The artist never had time to finish his work since he died of plague in 1631.

Left: *view of the cathedral presbytry with the main altar, and the apse vault with the mosaic depicting Christ Enthroned between the Virgin and St. John the Evangelist.*
Opposite page: *the interior of the cathedral.*

ECTO FALCOM S HABENTE HOC OPUS IN CURA NEC NON OPERE QUOQUE TUR HEST P

*T*he Pulpit in the Cathedral

Detail of the panel depicting the Slaughter of the Innocents; opposite page: *the pulpit by Giovanni Pisano.*

The most important work of art inside the Cathedral is the pulpit sculpted by Giovanni Pisano between 1302 and 1310. Giovanni definitely came under the influence of the Gothic style which, from the north, spread all over Europe; as a matter of fact, several art historians feel that he actually worked in France for some years. Nonetheless, Giovanni never forgot his origins. In this second period of Italian Medieval sculpture, he knowingly managed to express the ardent, passionate, and, due to historical circumstances, tragic nature of a whole city, country, and maybe even a people. With the advent of Giovanni Pisano, new horizons were opened up to Italian sculpture, i.e., all roads leading to the Renaissance were, once and for all, left free. Accentuating the expressive liberty his father Nicola loved so much, Giovanni Pisano created the magnificent figure of Hercules a completely pagan and nude figure. Perhaps no one before Giovanni was able to express himself in such terms. This is why it can be safely stated that Giovanni Pisano, the favorite son and pupil of the equally great Nicola Pisano of Baptistry Pulpit fame, set the way for the daring new naturalistic school, thus thrusting himself ahead of his time right up to the threshold of the Renaissance. And it is evident that Giovanni's realism is attained through the use of light and shadow contrasts charged with great dramatic tension and carried out with such immense skill that the artist has always been

considered one of the greatest of the Italian (and European) sculptors. During the following centuries, Giovanni's intensely pursued search for content will turn up again and again as the keynote in the works of Jacopo della Quercia, Donatello, and Michelangelo.

The upper part of the pulpit consists of nine panels illustrating stories from the New Testament. The first panel depicts the Annunciation and the Visitation, and above, the Birth of St. John the Baptist. The second one shows the Nativity of Christ and the third the Adoration of the Magi, while the fourth panel illustrates the Presentation at the Temple and the Flight into Egypt. The fifth panel represents the Slaughter of the Innocents. The Passion of Christ, initiated in the sixth panel, ends in the seventh with the Crucifixion. The eighth and ninth are filled with Last Judgment scenes. The lower section is largely composed of allegorical figures representing the virtues and credos of the Catholic faith. The torment, drama, and tragedy of Giovanni Pisano have been given confirmation in the world of today which is so very tormented, dramatic, and tragic. Just a few months before starting on his magnum opus, Giovanni was commissioned by the Scrovegni family, noblemen from Padua, to sculpt the figure of a gentle Virgin Mary. There in Padua Giovanni was able to make the acquaintance of two men who would soon stand out as greats in their respective fields: Giotto di Bondone, painter, and Dante Alighieri, writer and poet.

The Pulpit: the Nativity Panel

In this panel Giovanni Pisano attains great expressiveness conveyed with a sensitive, highly competent hand. Pisano endows his portrayal of the Virgin with a maternal look of infinite tenderness and sweetness towards her Son, thus revealing the artist's involvement in the human drama of Christ. Giovanni did not limit his attention solely to telling the Nativity story, as can be noted in his rendering of the lowly shepherds' awestruck reactions. The goodness of this simple folk is expressed in the dialogue of the shepherds who are overcome with astonishment before the great event, the birth of the Savior. In the silence of the sculpted night, a few humble shepherds serve as examples of great purity and humility in this masterpiece by Giovanni Pisano.

The Pulpit: the Crucifixion Panel

In this panel all the torment and tragedy of Giovanni's own soul, as well as of his people and country, are revealed. The sense of drama is communicated in large part by the anatomical emphasis given to Christ's body and the placement of the group of women, dominated by the Virgin overcome with suffering, beneath the Cross. The influence of French Gothic sculpture is felt in the artist's highly personal treatment of this very human drama.

The Pulpit: the Caryatid Figures

This well-known marble group depicting a woman borne by four caryatid figures while breast-feeding two infants is to be interpreted as an allegorical representation of the church: the personification of the church is giving life to the Old and New Testaments represented by the two children at her breast, while the caryatid figures stand for the four cardinal virtues. The artist's treatment of the allegory reveals a realism which is strictly Tuscan— the sobriety of the composition, the rhythm of the spaces, and the the monumentality of the figures recall Giotto's wonderful frescoes. Thus, the decorative part of the group is reduced to insignificant patterns which get lost in the vigorous, self-assured treatment of the famous marble figures. The group vibrates with life and spirituality, a sign of the artist's deep understanding of both sculptural and theological matters. We can only add that here Giovanni Pisano was way ahead of his times, foreshadowing Donatello and Michelangelo.

Galileo's Lamp

Midway down the nave hangs a cast bronze lamp executed by Vincenzo Possenti in 1586 after a design by G. B. Lorenzi. It is commonly known as " Galileo's lamp," since it is believed that the great scientist figured out the law of the pendulum by observing the lamp as it swung back and forth.

The Mosaics

The mosaic in its breathtaking majesty is reminiscent of the Venetian and Sicilian works in this artistic field. The latter in particular must have greatly influenced the numerous artists who worked on the mosaics in the Pisan Cathedral. The composition is rigid and contained in the best Eastern tradition and conveys that sense of mystery and spirituality which is typical of a large portion of Medieval painting. This is borne out by the figure of the Christ Pantocrater which, set amidst elaborate decorative motifs, is the undeniable center of attention. The refined treatment of the mosaic is outstanding for its rich color scheme and strong contrasts of light and shadow. The figure of St. John the Evangelist on the right has been attributed to Cimabue. Unfortunately, the work suffered damage in the Cathedral fire of 1595.

Two details of the mosaic over the apse depicting Christ Enthroned between the Virgin and St. John the Evangelist.

The Virgin and Child

The Tuscan Mannerist Antonio Sogliani (1491-1544) painted this version of a typical Raphaelesque subject, treating it with sweetness and elegance typical of Raphael's style.

St. Agnes

This is one of the most important and famous paintings inside the Cathedral. All of the elements characteristic of Renaissance painting are emphasized here: line, color, and atmosphere. Andrea del Sarto was a careful observer of Leonardo's technique, yet he never failed to add a personal touch to great technical skill. The poet Robert Browning dedicated a famous book to St. Agnes.

The Tomb of Henry VII of Luxembourg

The finest example of funerary art in the Cathedral is the tomb sculpted by Tino di Camaino for Emperor Henry VII of Luxembourg. The subjects of the sarcophagus reliefs derive from classical themes previously utilized by Giovanni Pisano who in turn had followed in the footsteps of his father, Nicola. The high relief of the figures and the strong contrast of light and shadow created by the movement of the twelve Apostle figures reveal the origins of this artist who is generally classified as the most faithful follower of the Pisan school.

Henry VII was proclaimed King of Germany in 1308, and was crowned Holy Roman Emperor in 1312 in Rome. Thus, when he died in Buonconvento near Siena in 1313, he was taken back to Pisa for burial. Dante even mentioned the melancholy young emperor in the Paradise section of the Divine Comedy. In the niche above, there are two refined angels by Domenico Ghirlandaio.

The Urn of St. Ranieri

The mortal remains of the patron saint of Pisa, St. Ranieri, have been collected in the big urn behind the altar in the chapel dedicated to him. The saint, who died in 1161, is still fervidly worshipped by the people of Pisa. Up until 1591 his remains had been preserved in a more modest sarcophagus; the one currently in use was sculpted in 1688 by G. B. Foggini. It is made of precious marbles donated by Cosimo III, the grand duke of Tuscany, and the grand duchess, Vittoria della Rovere. Every year, on June 17, the anniversary of the death of St. Ranieri, the urn is opened and the relics displayed for the veneration of the faithful.

Detail of the baptistry loggia decorated by Nicola Pisano; opposite page: ***the Baptistry.***

THE BAPTISTRY

The Baptistry is a grandiose circular building with a circumference of approximately 348 feet. If the statue of St. John the Baptist is counted, it turns out be several feet higher than the Leaning Tower. 34,000 Pisan families taxed themselves in order that the world's biggest baptistry be built. It was a common Italian custom to erect the baptistry separate from the main church building, possibly because the unbaptized, were not entitled to set foot inside the holy building. Our information regarding the various stages in construction is rather sketchy. On the other hand, the great differences between the Romanesque and Gothic styles on the building's exterior lead us to think that the work

was carried out off and on over a long period of time. It is certain that the first architect was Diotisalvi who in 1153 drew up plans and laid the foundations for the building. The Gothic decoration on the outside has been attributed to Giovanni Pisano who is known to have worked on the building between 1277-1284. The columns on either side of the main doorway are of classical inspiration unlike the other two small columns farther in which are of Byzantine derivation. Unknown Sicilian master craftsmen carved the architrave and the small panels set on either side of the doorway. The representations of the months of the year are interesting because of their simple expressive style.

The Interior of the Baptistry

" 1053 Mense Augusti fundata fuit haec...." reads the inscription on the first pilaster to the right of the Baptistry entranceway. The name " Diotisalvi magister...." may be found instead on the first pilaster to the left. In the center stands the stupendous Baptismal Font which was sculpted and set up by Guido Bigarelli da Como in 1246. The octagonal shape of the font seems to contrast with the perfectly circular form of the Baptistry which, incidentally, is the sole example of a round baptistry to be found anywhere in Italy. Children used to be baptized there by immersion in accordance with an old custom whereas adults were immersed in the huge central basin. Nowadays the font is still used, but the modern rite calls for sprinkling. Bigarelli's font is embellished with marvelous marble inlays which may be admired in perfect condition on the outside of the work. The statue of St. John the Baptist in the middle of the font is a fine contemporary work by Italo Griselli. Thus the 20th century too has left its mark in the Baptistry of Pisa. The acoustical effects produced by the dome's perfectly round shape is of great interest. The Baptistry guards can demonstrate them.

Left: *St. John the Baptist by Italo Griselli;* below: *the baptismal font by Guido Bigarelli da Como.* Opposite page: *the interior of the baptistry.*

The Baptistry Pulpit

This pulpit was carved by Nicola Pisano. Although the great sculptor's origins are a hornet's nest of controversy, we know for sure that he was born sometime early in the 13th century and that he died after 1278. His masterpiece, the pulpit in the Pisa Baptistry, was sculpted between 1255 and 1260. And no matter where Nicola Pisano was born, Pisans are proud to call him " Sculptore de Pisis" for it was only in Pisa that he reached his extraordinary artistic maturity. "Masterpiece" does not entirely do justice to the pulpit which seems to embody the very spirit of the man who would be called " the greatest innovator of Italian sculpture." No one before Nicola was able to give such a meaningful, and thus in effect Renaissance, sense to the art of sculpture: while at the same time other Romanesque artists were in large part closely tied and subordinate to architecture, Nicola Pisano removed his figures from the Romanesque sphere by endowing them with life and movement and thus a completely new spirit. Love for his country, the unforgettable grandeur that was Rome and thus his own city " Colonia Julia obsequens" were the factors which drove Nicola to passionately study the classical forms of Roman sculpture. For this reason the Virgins carved by Nicola's hand recall the majestic matrons and goddesses of ancient Greece and Rome, especially in the first two panels of the pulpit which depict the Nativity and the Adoration of the Magi.

Just below, between the two panels, the nude male figure standing on top of the capital, is a detail of huge interest. This figure representing Hercules was not meant by the sculptor to be an accurate anatomical study of the human body, since evidently the time was not yet ripe. But Nicola was clearly attempting to express himself in a

Two details of the pulpit panels portraying the Presentation in the Temple (above) and the Adoration of the Magi (right).

new way, in a way no one else before him had ever done, and even today his maturity and freedom of expression provoke reactions of wonder in the viewer. The other panels representing the " Presentation at the Temple, the "Crucifixion" and the "Last Judgement" are equally outstanding and it stands to reason that seven hundred years later Nicola Pisano's greatness still lives on. Nicola, like man of today, was constantly caught up in attempts to say and create something new using the greatest freedom of artistic expression. Nicola made sculpture look different because he really had something new to say, just like the great artists who followed in his iconoclastic footsteps: Giovanni Pisano, Jacopo della Quercia, Donatello, and Michelangelo.

The Pulpit: the Nude Hercules

That classical art had an enormous influence on both the personality and art of Nicola Pisano is borne out in full by this "anatomic" Hercules. With his instinctive love of freedom as a citizen of a free republic, Nicola defied his own times·by not heeding the attempts to render the world around him colorless and static. It was Nicola's limpid, serene outlook which dominated the 13th century unopposed. With his Hercules, the great sculptor deliberately returned to classical forms by echoing the motifs of the archeological remains he had so lovingly studied, especially in the Phaedra Sarcophagus and the big Greek Baccanal Vase, both in the Camposanto. Thus, the reverent superstitions surrounding the pagan world fell away way forever while, at the same time, an enormous stimulus for advancement in the Italian, cultural and perhaps European, Middle Ages was exerted. Without heeding his critics and mindless of controversy since no great mind purposely seeks out controversy, Nicola Pisano created his Hercules to cry out to the world with his free spirit i.e. the great cultural independence of a lively, restless, and modern mind.

Portico of the Museo dell'Opera del Duomo with the busts from the outer loggia of the Baptistry.

THE MUSEO DELL'OPERA DEL DUOMO

The building that houses the Museo dell'Opera del Duomo stands on the southwest corner of the grassy and solitary Piazza dei Miracoli. The view from the upper loggia extending around the ancient cloister is truly spectacular. It creates a wonderful visual and emotional link with the artworks housed here and the monuments from which they originated.

The buildings, originally erected as the residence for the cathedral's canons (who lived there from about 1100 to the early XVII century) was later used for different purposes. Its current configuration dates from the early seventeenth century when it was completely remodelled to house the Seminario Arcivescovile. Later it passed to private ownership, then in 1784 it became the headquarters of the academy of fine arts, and home of Giovanni Rosini, great man of letters. In 1887 it was taken over by the Cappuccine Sisters and became a cloistered convent.

Finally, in 1979 it was purchased by the Opera della Primaziale in order to create a true Museo dell'Opera. It was opened in 1986, and through its treasures and artworks, it tells visitors the long and complex story of the Primaziale Pisana and its famous monuments together with the city's cultural and artistic history.

The oldest and most famous nucleus of the museum's collections are located on the ground floor and in the portico. These are sculptures from the XII to XVII century, including the masterpieces by Nicola and Giovanni Pisano, Tino di Camaino and Nino Pisano. The Tesoro del Duomo, or Cathedral Treasure, is in a separate room and in the adjacent chapel. It comprises liturgical items and precious objects from the Medieval cathedral including Giovanni Pisano's ivory Madonna and silverware dating from the XVI to XIX centuries. The rest of the museum is arranged more or less in chronological and systematic order: on the first floor there are sculptures dating from the XVI to the XIX centuries, wooden intarsias from the Renaissance, illuminated Medieval choir-books, sacred paraments, liturgical garments and cloths, a collection of Egyptian, Etruscan and Roman objects and finally a graphic section with famous XIX century engravings by Carlo Lasinio, first curator of the Camposanto Monumentale (the Monumental Cemetery).

The Islamic Bronzes: the Griffon and the Basin

The relationships between Pisa, the maritime city and the Orient, land of the heathens was always difficult, strife ridden, and yet there was always secret admiration which can be symbolized in the Islamic items that are believed to have been captured as war booty.

The echo of the great voyages to the East, of relations with a distant, alien world, the memory of fierce battles and long military expeditions, but also perhaps of peaceful trade are clearly heard in these items that are displayed not only as victory trophies but also as special souvenirs. They are a lasting remembrance of important and valuable contacts with a culturally rich civilization.

It is in this light that the two Islamic pieces should be viewed and studied, they are the cast bronze basin and Fatimid griffon.

The griffon is a monumental statue dating from the XII century, and up until the late XIX century it stood atop the typanum of the cathedral's apse, that is the most important and visually striking position for those who came to the heart of the city. Little is known about this superb piece. And it matters less if it was taken as booty during the crusades, during the Balearic expedition or if it was the gift of some Arabian prince. One thing is sure, its powerful shape is typical of Iranian Islamic art.

The other famous piece is the metal basin with the fine engraved decorations. There are inscriptions along the edge and zoomorphic figures in medallions. It too is very old and perhaps dates from Seljuk dynasty (XII century); it is exceptionally crafted and is the focus of great attention for scholars in this field.

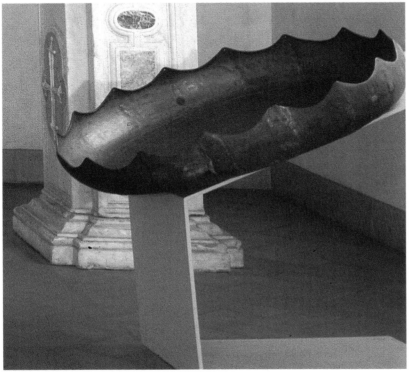

The Headless Female Statues

Giovanni Pisano's artistic skill virtually bursts from the two Verrucano marble blocks carved into the figures of two headless girls.

The first is a beautiful female figure holding a vase in her left hand; the right arm is missing. The forms are balanced and move around a vertical axis that supports the figure as she steps forward. It is harmonious and light, with a uniquely graceful sense of motion.

The other statue is vibrant with life, spontaneity and movement. Giovanni's mastery comes through as the girl slightly raises her skirts to dance.

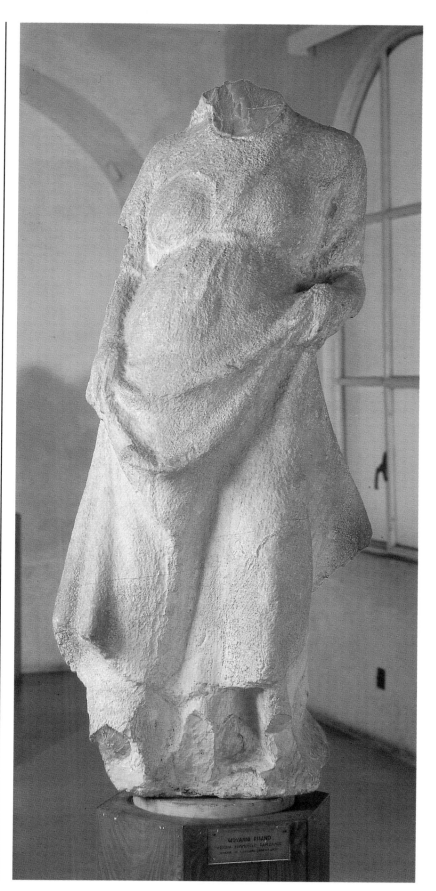

The Wooden Christ from the Cathedral

This monumental colored wood carving of Christ is truly worthy of admiration. Until the disastrous fire of 1595 it hung in the cathedral presbytry.

It is probably datable around the second half of the XII century and can certainly be identified as a Deposed Christ. It was part of a group similar to the ones in the Pieve at Vicopisano and in the Volterra cathedral.

Notwithstanding an old legend reported by Pisan historians saying that the Christ was brought from the Holy Land, this magnificent crucified figure, with its stark beauty and lines requiring little decoration, is French.

It is one of the greatest masterpieces of period sculpture, especially for its fine proportions and shapes. It possesses a charm of its own which is accentuated by the contrast between the plastic masses of diagonal broken rhythms that delineate Christ's body against the cross giving it drama and pathos, and the fine, subtle sculpting seemingly carved with the tip of a chisel that delicately embroiders the surface.

It is sufficient to note the decided and elegant folds of the loin-cloth, the ribs that are just visible on the chest, and the solemn face, filled with humanity's suffering. Then there is a clear contrast with the stylized lines of the elongated limbs. All this makes it easier to understand that this Deposed Crhist, with its majestic, solemn beauty, with its profound asceticism and spirituality can be classed among the masterpieces of Burgundian sculpture.

The Virgin of the Smile

This may be one of Giovanni Pisano's earliest carvings of the Virgin (1280 circa). It reveals a. clear break with the classic dignity and serene solemnity of Nicola Pisano's style, and a definite Gothic imprint.

The Infant Jesus, is absorbed in a loving, silent coversation with His Mother. Her arm holds him safely and the entire motion of the statue seems to be directing his gaze upwards.

It was with the subject of the silent conversations of gazes (hence statue's other title the Virgin of the Conversation) that Giovanni Pisano managed to imbue the relationship between the Mother and Son with new psychological and spiritual meanings.

This is how the elegant profile of this Madonna represents the most plastic, human and definite expression of a Mother who adores her child and in turn is loved by him.

The Ivory Madonna

The Ivory Madonna, carved by Giovanni Pisano around the end of the XIII century is one of the most famous and prized works in the museum.

By cleverly using the natural curves of the elephant tusk, the artist managed to create a highly dynamic sculpture without diminishing its stately-sacred meaning. In fact the dynamism blends perfectly with the refined elegance of the artist's mastery

THE ETRUSCAN LION

The origins of the lion set atop the Medicean walls are shrouded in mystery. Some art historians claim that the work is definitely Etruscan, while others feel that it is an Oriental-influenced Romanesque piece. What is certain is that the impressive strength of this lion figure revealed by its powerful lines and great size suggests the fabulous age when economic prosperity and trade were the keynotes of the city's (and state's) political life.

THE JEWISH CEMETERY AND SYNAGOGUE

Once upon a time there was a Jewish cemetery in the Porta Nova neighborhood, but starting from the 18th century, the Jewish community took up burying their dead in this corner of peace and quiet. Pisa's name was both respected and feared in the far off Oriental lands during the Middle Ages, and naturally numerous Pisans had dealings with the Jewish communities in these countries. Documents indicate that the first Jews actually living in Pisa settled along the secluded " Chiasso dei Giudei " (" Street of the Hebrews ") starting from 1165. Then during the 14th and 15th centuries, the Pisan Jews grew very important in the city's financial world as bankers and in 1492 Jews fleeing from the Spanish Inquisition found refuge in Pisa. The next centuries witnessed

The interior of the synagogue.

even greater advances; in fact, by the late 19th century the Pisan Jewish community numbered approximately one thousand. Active in both the business and intellectual circles of the city, the Pisan Jews gave strong impetus to industries, especially the textile branch. Renowned scientists belonging to the Jewish community of Pisa were acclaimed by the Italian state for their great contributions to the whole country. Only under Fascism did the racial laws lead to the break up of the community, and it was a terrible loss for the whole city. Today there is only a tiny religious community of Jews who are faithful guardians of a heritage and religious tradition they are deeply proud of. Pisan Jews have been coming to meditate and pray for here in the synagogue over two hundred years.

THE CAMPOSANTO MONUMENTAL CEMETERY

The last monument to be built in Piazza dei Miracoli was the Monumental Cemetery, called " Camposanto " in Italian. The architect entrusted with the project, Giovanni di Simone, began work in 1278. Here, along the roofed-in passageways, the most-deserving and best-known Pisans receive burial even today. Work was broken off in 1284 because of the war against Genoa which led to the naval defeat of August 6 of the same year. Giovanni di Simone, like thousands of other Pisans, met his death in the tragic battle and thus found a final resting place in the Mediterranean Sea not far from his beloved city. Therefore, the Camposanto was finished much later when the Gothic style had already been deprived of its original purity. In 1464, once the ornamentation was added to the arcading, construction was finally completed. On July 27, 1944 two foreign armies fighting a war begun a long time before came to arms in Pisa and the ensuing battle was bitter and hard-fought. Men from countries with different cultural backgrounds, from other civilizations did not realize the universal importance of the monuments in Piazza dei Miracoli. That day angry artillery shots were aimed at the Camposanto and the resulting damage was enormous. The roof was totally destroyed and, in the huge fire started by cannon shots which followed, the lead roofcovering melted and seeped down through the frescoes, which were seriously damaged. It looked as though the noble Camposanto which had been a source of inspiration to Christina of Sweden, Franz Liszt, and Theophil Gauthier among other greats, would be lost forever. Italian and foreign artlovers were heartbroken at the loss of the world famous monument. And so, in 1945, a huge restoration project aimed mainly at fixing up the frescoes was begun and has continued practically until today. By now it is easy to see that the Camposanto is once more as it had been before.

Although the famous frescoes were started in 1360, the cycle was completed only three centuries later. The fresco technique is the Italian invention for decorating walls. The first step in the process is to coat the wall with a layer of lime mixed with coarse-grained sand. Then another layer of lime, this time with fine-grained sand mixed in, is placed on top. The preliminary drawing called the " sinopia " is sketched onto this second layer. The last step is the addition of color to a third layer of thick lime and fine-grained sand which gradually covers the sinopia outline. It is obvious that the latter disappears from view leaving only the fresco showing. After the terrible experience the frescoes went through during the war, they were detached from the walls by means of a new, avantgarde technique.

The Monumental Cemetery, Camposanto, from the outside.

The Tabernacle of the Campo Santo

A graceful Gothic decoration of the Monumental Cemetery, the tabernacle breaks up the almost too unitary. lines of the immense structure. Inside is the Virgin enthroned between four saints and a kneeling figure. The work may have been done by a follower of Giovanni Pisano during the second half of the XIV century because it recalls the master's inimitable grace.

The Bombardment of the Campo Santo

It was close to the end of World War II, on 27 July 1944 that Pisa was stricken by continuous bombing raids and a bomb fell on the roof of the Campo Santo. It caused a horrible fire which, due to the lack of equipment, no one could extinguish. The lead roof melted and oozed down the side of the building like lava, destroying priceless masterpieces. We owe much to the dedication and spirit of sacrifice of those who worked to rebuild and restore this great monument that seemed to have been lost forever.

Preceding pages: *view of the courtyard inside the Camposanto with the dome of the Dal Pozzo Chapel.*

Left: *the dome of the Dal Pozzo Chapel;* below: *two statues in the Northern Gallery.*
Opposite page, from the top: *Roman sarcophagus and classic sarcophagus with scenes from the story of Phaedra and Hippolytus* (Northern Gallery)

*T*he Chains

This is all that is left of the chains which were once used to close off the city's harbor. Carried off as trophies of war by the Florentines and Genoese during their naval excursions against Pisa, they were spontaneously returned to the city once Italian independence was won.

The Sarcophagi

Inside the Camposanto there are a number of Roman sarcophagi from various periods which were excavated in Pisa and placed here at the beginning of the 19th century. The most interesting sarcophagus to be found in the northern corridor was used in 1076 to receive the remains of Matilda, the Countess of Tuscany. Decorated with Greco-Roman reliefs, the so-called Phaedra sarcophagus deserves our closest attetion. Like most other sarcophagi of the same period, i.e. the 2nd century A. D., the subject illustrated in the reliefs is of mythological origin. Briefly, the legend of Phaedra tells the story of a highly sensual woman, who perversely cast off her husband in favor of her husband's own son, Hippolytus. Nevertheless, Hippolytus never gave in to his stepmother who, furious at being rejected, then accused him of having raped her. Hippolytus was punished with death and Phaedra with such remorse that she hanged herself. This typically Greek tragedy has inspired artists and writers from Euripides and Sophocles to Racine and D'Annunzio. The reliefs on the Phaedra sarcophagus give the impression of a pagan world in which Roman art is gradually drawing away from reality. In fact, by this time, we are well into the Early Christian period when the transformation of the classical world was taking place, and this disintegration meant stylized, concise treatment where sculpture was concerned. Nicola Pisano was familiar with this work and was influenced by it when he started work on his marvelous Baptistry pulpit in 1255.

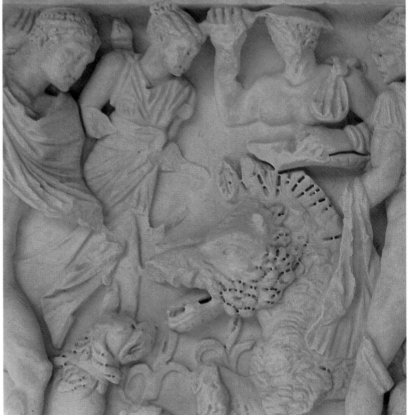

Detail of the Triumph of Death, with the scene of the Cavalcade.

The Frescoes

Not all the frescoes are on display, as many of them are still inside the Dal Pozzo Chapel here in the Camposanto. At present works by the following masters are exhibited: Taddeo Gaddi, Piero di Puccio, Spinello Aretino, and Benozzo Gozzoli, who was the greatest and most famous artist ever to have worked inside the Camposanto (the main hall off the north corridor is also dedicated to Gozzoli). Of particular interest are the Florentine master's sinopias and studies. But we must go on to the next large hall to be able to experience that terrifing yet meaningful allegorical work by an unknown 14th century Pisan artist which illustrates the Triumph of Death, the Last Judgement, and Hell. The Anacoreti della Tebaide fresco pales with respect to dramatic effect when compared to this .work. In the group of three frescoes the Medieval drama unfolds in all its tragedy. Everything is animated by religious fervor and by such a pessimistic outlook on life that it is shocking to look at them even now: first, Death not Life triumphs over the destiny of man. Then man must stand to be judged in the Last Judgement to receive his eternal reward or punishment. Lastly, punishment naturally brings on the apocalyptic vision of Hell with its endless suffering and pain.

Detail of the Last Judgement.

Detaching Frescoes

First of all, an extremely thin layer of canvas treated with animal glue solubile in very hot water is applied to the fresco. After a preliminary drying period, the canvas is literally torn away, hence the name of this process which is known as the " tearing technique". Together with the canvas, the first layer of color is also detached. Clearly in this case we cannot see the color since only the reverse side is facing us. Therefore, the fresco which has undergone this treatment is then placed on huge panels made of eternit braced by wooden supports and covered with extremely fine cotton gauze. Eternit is a modern prefabricated material composed of cement and abestos which does not react chemically or mechanically. The canvas containing the fresco is first pasted on these eternit panels using cold glue and then removed with a solvent solution. Thus, the fresco is once more visible. The sinopias, or preliminary drawings, often reappear when the fresco is torn off the wall. These sinopias are of the greatest importance since practically all of them were executed by the master himself, whereas all the frescoes are the work of pupils. It cannot be denied that the liberty of expression, the purity of line, and extraordinary dynamism which animate the preliminary sketches are tangible proof of the high level attained by the artists. Thus, during the final restoration, the Camposanto sinopias were detached by the same technique as the one used on the frescoes so that they could be seen by visitors and art historians alike in the halls of the monumental cemetery.

The entrance to the Museo delle Sinopie.

THE MUSEUM OF THE SINOPIAS

The Museum of the Sinopias is currently housed in a wing of the old Ospedale di Misericordia that was built to designs by Giovanni di Simone between 1257 and 1286, before the monumental cemetery. Then it was expanded during the first half of the XIV century along the south side of Piazza del Duomo.

A curious historical episode, that took place on the Tyrrhenian coast in 1241 is closely linked to the construction of this hospital. Some ships that were carrying cardinals to Rome for a conclave the pope had called in order to depose the Emperor Frederick II were captured by the Ghibelline fleet. Therefore the pope, Gregory IX, excommunicated the entire city; his writ was only revoked when the Pisans laid the first stone of the hospital to repent publicly for their grave error.

Although the building was greatly remodelled over the years, and mainly in the XIX century, it is still fascinating. The long, broad, brick and stone façade completes the perspective of Piazza dei Miracoli, and comprises an elegant setting for the rows of stalls filled with colorful wares that attract tourists seeking souvenirs of the city.

After considerable restorations that have preserved and maintained the building's original structure, the existing museum was inaugurated in 1979. It contains the sinopias from the monumental cemetery.

Sinopias are the preparatory drawings for frescoes done directly on the wall; one of the explanations for the development of this technique is the lack of large quantities of paper or other similar materials during the XIV century.

The drawings were done in small size, directly onto the next to the last coat of plaster called "arriciato".

The artists used a brush dipped into a red-earth pigment (actually they also used greenish yellow pigments and charcoal) from Sinope, a city in Asia Minor, and hence the name "sinopia".

These drawings were then covered with a layer of rough and fine sand called "grassello" onto which the colors were applied. When the work was complete the sinopias, evidently were permanently hidden.

They became visible following a tragic event. During War II, an incendiary bomb exploded on the Campo on the night of 27 July 1944. The ensuing fire destroyed most of the frescoes; the few that remained were in such poor condition that they had to be removed for restoration. As they were being taken off, the lovely preliminary drawings once again saw the light. Now, using the same techniques applied in fresco restoration, the sinopias are fixed onto eternit slabs and are displayed in a separate gallery.

The sinopias are extremely important in terms of Medieval art because they were done by the great mas-

The Annunciation by Benozzo Gozzoli, detail.

ters themselves. The frescoes, on the other hand, were actually painted by the masters' pupils and assistants. The sinopias, therefore, are expressive and free, they have a freshness of line and spontaneity of composition and execution that are the tangible fruits of great artistic talent.

The Upper Floor

The museum is arranged on two levels: the upper is dedicated to the panels with the most interesting and oldest sinopias, that is the Holy Fathers, the Last Judgement, Hell and the famous "Triumph of Death". They were all done by an unknown artist dubbed the "Master of the Triumph of Death". His true identity, Buonamico Buffalmacco was discovered by the art critic Luciano Bellosi in the 'fifties.

This great Florentine artist drew his figures with a firm hand that made elegant, clean lines. In the long panel of the Triumph of Death, they seem to spring from the rough plaster surface. It is sufficient to look at the purity of the expression on the faces, the fine outlines of the horses and other animals, the great battle between the angels and demons to understand that we are looking at the work of a truly great artist. In the rather uniform panorama of fourteenth century painting that was dominated by Giotto's influence, Buffalmacco seems to have struck out on his own, instead of blindly following the great master 's rules, and thereby partially renewed the traditions by working from within. It is interesting to compare the sinopia with the fresco. One can see the changes, the artist's "second opinion", details that were eliminated in the final version. In brief, the whole, painstaking process of fresco. and sketch are there, the basis of a fresco cycle the zenith of the Medieval world's artistic achievement.

This impression is confirmed by looking at the sinopias of the Ascension, with the traditional Christ in the mandorla, carried by four angels. In the drawing the figure has a spiritual and yet profoundly human beauty and a severe grace that was partly hidden by the colors added when the fresco was painted.

The sinopia of the Crucifixion is located on the eastern wall on the same floor. It was the first great fresco cycle (1320-30) by the Pisan artist Francesco Traini. Although the central part of the sinopia is missing, the composition is still clearly legible. A careful analysis reveals the artist's great skill acquired through lessons from Simone Martini and Lippo Memmi perhaps even more than the finished fresco.

It is sufficient to look at the figure of Christ on the Cross. It was drawn diagonally to add strength to the composition, and the facial features. Even in death they remained gentle, the face is drooping on the chest; the stomach is drawn in to emphasize the suffering. The angels with spread wings, are blinded with pain and seem to flutter madly around the Cross. Below, the figures of the onlookers, drawn with curving, continuous lines not to break up the rhythms, seem to participate in this great collective drama.

On the northern wall, there are small sinopias by four of the greatest painters who worked in Florence during

The Triumph of Death, detail.

the XIV century. Taddeo Gaddi was Giotto's favorite pupil, and although he continued with the master's pictorial lines, he did additional studies on perspective and created the Stories of Job. Andrea Bonaiuti, created the Stories of St. Ranier; Spinello Aretino painted the Stories of St. Efisio and Potito. He was still a member of Giotto's school, but the fourteenth century was drawing to a close, and he continued by enlivening the tradition with brilliant innovations. The fourth great artist was Antonio Veneziano who developed an intelligent bond between the traditional school of Giotto and the Bolognese world of miniature.

The collection on the upper floor ends with the large sinopia of the Ptolemaic Cosmography, that is the Birth of the Universe. It is presented in a series of concentric circles clearly influence by Ptolemy and Augustine; it was executed by Piero di Puccio da Orvieto, an artist known solely for his fresco cycle in the Campo Santo (the drawings for the Coronation of the Vrgin and the first Stories of Genesis) can be seen on the ground floor. These works reveal his brilliant taste for architectural compositions where careful attention to space and proportions blends with strange deformities in the perspective.

The groundfloor room.

The Groundfloor

The sinopias by Benozzo Gozzoli are located on the groundfloor; these works are totally different as to nature and meaning when compared with those on the first floor.

By the time Gozzoli was painting, paper was much more readily available; therefore, artists no longer had to draw sinopias directly onto the wall.

The wall thus became an enormous sketchbook, where the master and his pupils "jotted down" their ideas for the arrangement and composition of the fresco.

This is why these sinopias are particularly fascinating:

they are sketches filled with references to daily life. They transport us back in time and provide priceless information about the artist's techniques. He used mathematics and geometry to develop the large, complex perspective, and also to outline the human figures. The tour of the museum ends with an interesting collection of watercolored drawings by Giampaolo Lasinio, son of the Monumental Cemetery's first curator . These pictures give a clear and precise idea of what Europe's greatest XIV and XV fresco cycle looked like before it was damaged.

Portrait of Galileo Galilei by Sustermans.
Opposite page, above: **the balls that Galilei used for his studies on gravity;** below from the left: **Galileo's birth certificate and the Galilean telescope (Museum of Science, Florence).**

Page 72 and 73: **Trajan's Baths, known as Nero's Baths**

Galileo Galilei (1564-1642)

Galileo was born in Pisa on February 15, 1564, most likely in the working class neighborhood of Sant' Andrea fuori Porta. He completed his studies of philosophy and mathematics at the University of Pisa. It was inside the Cathedral of Pisa that Galileo, while observing the bronze lamp above the nave as it swung back and forth, figured out the law of the isochronism of the pendulum. Several years later, from the Leaning Tower, he carried out experiments on weights, proving that when two weights are dropped from the same height they fall at the same speed. Galileo's experiments principally involved physics and astronomy and from 1592-1610 he taught at the University of Padua. Between 1608-1609 a device called the " eyeglass " whose purpose was to make faraway objects seem closer was in use in nearby Venice. Galileo worked on this instrument and transformed it into what would later be called the Galilean telescope. He made a number of important discoveries studying the heavens with his telescope — he discovered the seas and mountains on the moon and four satellites of Jupiter which he dubbed " Medicean stars " after the Medicis of Florence. On March 12, 1610 in Venice he wrote and published " Sidereus Nuncius " which made public his discoveries and in July of the same year Cosimo II de'

Medici appointed him First Mathematician of the University of Pisa without compulsory residence and teaching duties. After eighteen happy years at Padua he moved to Arcetri just outside Florence. In 1632 he published his " Dialogue on the Major Systems" in which he expressed his agreement with and confirmation of Copernicus's theories that the earth is round and that the earth revolves around the sun. This work is a milestone in the history of scientific thought. It was not just a simple tract on astronomy and physics but a work which served to eliminate all the prejudices and false notions held by official science of the day and one which indicated the scientific method to be used in the study of nature and our planet as well as other heavenly bodies. The publication of this study brought on the wrath of the College of Rome which ordered Galileo to appear before the Holy Inquisition on April 12, 1633. On June 22 of that year, after having submitted to endless interrogations and threats, Galileo, at this point bitter and morally worn out, was forced to retract his work. In December he obtained permission to return to Arcetri where on, January 8, 1642, at the age of seventy-eight, he died blind and exiled.

The façade of the church of Santa Caterina on the square with the same name; left: *detail of the rose window.* Opposite page, top: *Virgin and Child, mosaic in the lunette over the portal;* below, from the left: *monument to the Archibishop Simone Saltarelli by Nino Pisano and the stained glass window inside the church.*

SANTA CATERINA

The Church of Santa Caterina was built upon the express desire of St. Dominick around 1220 and was dedicated to St. Catherine because it was here in Pisa that she received the Stigmata. In 1311 the great Sienese artist Simone Martini painted one of his masterpieces, an altarpiece depicting the Virgin and Child with saints for this church. The famous painting is now in the National Museum of Pisa.

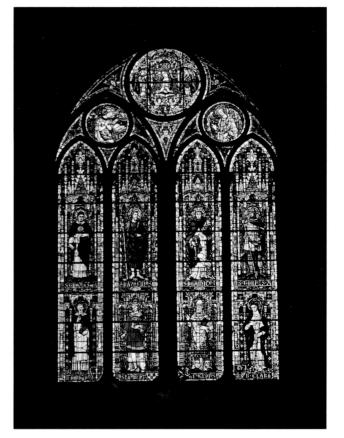

THE ABBEY OF SAN ZENO

This building, together with the adjoining Camaldolese Monastery, was already built by the 10th century. Damaged during World War II, it was restored. The faithful restoration brought to light its lovely, harmonious architecture dating from various periods.

The Abbey of San Zeno.

Palazzo dei Cavalieri, or della Carovana;
right: *the statue of Cosimo I de' Medici
by Pietro Francavilla*

PIAZZA
DEI CAVALIERI

Piazza dei Cavalieri is one of the loveliest and most harmonious squares in Italy. It occupies the site of the
Roman forum which during the Middle Ages became
the city's political center where the Pisans used to hold
democratic meetings to debate matters involving the
free city state. Here in this square the Republic's triumphs and victories were celebrated, although here
too in 1406 the Commissariat of the Republic
announced the end of Pisan independence. Today the
square retains its Renaissance appearance. In 1561
Cosimo I de' Medici, Grand duke of Tuscany, founded
the religious-military order of Santo Stefano, on whose
behalf the Church of the Cavalieri was erected between
1565-1569. The design is the work of Giorgio Vasari
and various other Florentine architects who worked
with him. It is the sole Renaissance church in a city
where Romanesque is the unchallenged master. Inside
are several Turkish flags captured during fierce naval
battles and carried back to Pisa as war trophies by the

Knights of the Order of Saint Stephen. On October 7, 1571 the knights fought bravely in the Battle of Lepanto, earning glory in a battle which would prove decisive for all of Christianity. The building situated near the Church of the Cavalieri was renovated by Giorgio Vasari and the façade decorations are the work of Vasari and his pupils. The building, which was originally the knights' military training quarters, now houses the Scuola Normale Superiore, the institute of higher education founded by Napoleon in 1810. The Scuola Normale, which is totally separate from the University of Pisa, is unique in Italy in that only the best, hand-picked students are admitted to its courses. Many famous men have studied here: for instance, the first Italian to win the Nobel Prize (in 1906), the great modern poet, Giosue Carducci, was a student. But undoubtedly the best known alumni of the Scuola Normale are the physicists Enrico Fermi and Bruno Pontecorvo who were friends as well as classmates. After the war, Pontecorvo emigrated to Russia while Fermi stayed in the United States where they had both worked. There in December 1942 Fermi successfully produced a controlled nuclear reaction for the first time in a laboratory.

Opposite: *the arms of the Knights of St. Stephen;* below, from the left: *two busts of the Grand Dukes of Tuscany in the oval niches on the façade of the Palazzo dei Cavalieri.*

Detail of the façade of the Palazzo dei Cavalieri;
below: ***Palazzo dell'Orologio.***

The façade of the church of Santo Stefano dei Cavalieri.

SANTO STEFANO DEI CAVALIERI

Cosimo I de' Medici, Grand Duke of Tuscany, commissioned the construction of the Church of Santo Stefano right over the former Church of San Sebastiano. The great Florentine architect Vasari, began work on Santo Stefano's in 1565. Four years later the church was consecrated.

Inside the building there are several noteworthy works by Vasari himself (he was also a painter) and Fancelli to whom the pulpit has been attributed. In addition, there are a number of Turkish flags hung about the walls of the church brought to Pisa as trophies of war. The magnificent main altar is of great note. Commissioned by Grand Duke Cosimo III it is made of precious marbles and Oriental red porphyry. The mortal remains of St. Stephen, donated by Pope Innocent XII to Cosimo III, are preserved in this altar and in 1427, Donatello sculpted an exceptional goldplated copper statue of St. Rossore for it. The statue is in the back part of the altar set in a niche.

SAN FRANCESCO

The Church of San Francesco was begun during the second half of the 13th century and finished when the façade was completed at the beginning of the 14th. The building has been attributed to Nicola or Giovanni Pisano, even though there is no documentation to support this theory.

Right: *detail of the outside of the church of San Francesco;* below: *the interior.*

The façade of the church of San Sisto; left: *the interior.*

SAN SISTO

San Sisto is a very old, very simple Pisan Romanesque church begun on August 6, 1070, St. Sixtus' day on the religious calendar, and for this reason dedicated to him. In 1786 the church was in large part restored. While the effect on its antique, simple exterior was negligible, the inside, was tastelessly modified.

SAN FREDIANO

This is a very old church dating from XI-XIII centuries, however, it was greatly remodelled in the sixteen hundreds. The façade is simply decorated with a series of arches in the lower part and a double lighted window above. Inside there are some sixteenth century canvases, a XIII century crucifix and a Byzantine style Virgin and Child from the XIII century which is in the sacristy.

Right: *the façade of the church of San Frediano;*
below: *the interior.*

The historical Aula Magna in the University; left: the inscription dedicated to the poet Giosué Carducci, in the loggia of the courtyard at Sapienza.

THE UNIVERSITY

The first Law School was already active in Pisa by the 12th century, whereas the School of Medicine was opened only in the 13th. Then the University of Pisa was recognized by Pope Clement VI in 1343 and by Emperor Charles IV in 1350. The building currently occupied by the university was built in 1493 and later altered in 1550. Galileo studied and taught in these halls and it was here that he laid the foundations for modern experimental physics.

THE CAMPANO TOWER

The " Campano " received this nickname from the huge bell inside the tower that rises near the food market. Since the 18th century the bell has been used to summon the students to their lessons in the nearby university.

THE ALLA GIORNATA PALACE

This building first belonged to the Lanfreducci family. An outstanding example of Renaissance civil architecture it is now University headquarters.

The Campano Tower; below: ***Palazzo "alla Giornata".***

THE AGOSTINI PALACE

Built during the first part of the 15th century, the Agostini Palace also known as the Hussar's Palace is one of the oldest in the city. The building is made of terracotta and decorated with Gothic motifs.

The 15th century brought greater refinement to Pisan life. Elegant palaces symbolizing the new times replaced the old fashioned tower houses which stood for strength and solidity—the Agostini Palace, as we mentioned before, was one of the first of these new style residences to go up. Restored, the palace still exhudes its old splendor; its serene, elegant lines give the street flanking the river a particularly distinctive look. In addition, just as a number of other buildings in the city, the palace tilts to the right due to Pisa's friable ground conditions. At present the ground floor is occupied by the Ussero Cafe, opened in 1794, which has been a meeting place for generations of students from the nearby university.

THE TOSCANELLI PALACE

This building formerly belonged to the Lanfranchi family. In the 16th century it was restored by its new owners, the Toscanelli family and some claim that Michelangelo designed the façade. From 1821 to 1822 Lord Byron took up residence in the building and it was here that he wrote a part of his poem Don Juan. During the same time Shelley lived in a building directly opposite the Toscanelli Palace on the other side of the river which unfortunately was destroyed during World War II.

*The church of San Matteo and the entrance
to the Museo Nazionale.*

Following pages: *the cloister of the Museo Nazionale
di San Matteo.*

THE SAN MATTEO NATIONAL MUSEUM

The Pisa National Museum is undoubtedly one of the most interesting in all Italy and possibly in Europe. A number of the works housed here are unique —just the museum's Giovanni Pisanos and Andrea Pisanos alone would be enough to bestow fame on any museum. Of particular note are the works classified as the Pisan primitive school: Giunta Pisano and the great Master of San Martino are represented by exceptional paintings. These early Pisans are undoubtedly precursors of Cimabue from Florence and Duccio di Buoninsegna of Siena.

Simone Martini painted this extraordinary altarpiece in 1313 for the Church of Santa Caterina. It is definitely one of the finest works to have come out of Italian 14th century painting. Another fine piece is Nino Pisano's extremely sensitive and unusual sculpture entitled the " Madonna del Latte. " Last but certainly not least, we find the powerful St.Paul by Masaccio.

Crucifix by Giunta Pisano

Giunta Pisano was born near Pisa at the beginning of the 13th century and was active between 1229 and 1254. Only a tiny number of Giunta Pisano's works exist in the world. This particular painting in the Pisa National Museum (which incidentally is one of the few signed) is a splendid expression, or interpretation if you will, of profound dramatic tension It characterizes Pisano as one of the greatest of the Romanesque painters, and the most masterly interpreter of Christ the Man, the man who suffers with the greatest humility and realism (Christus Patiens).

Crucifix by Berlinghieri

Berlinghiero Berlinghieri, the master painter from Lucca, may be considered the ideal interpreter of the Christus Triumphans. A 13th century artist, he looked back to the highly spiritual tradition of Byzantine art with its mysticism and stern asceticism. The work on display in the National Museum, conveys a strong feeling of purification and spirituality.

Opposite page: **Virgin and Child and scenes from her life by Maestro di San Martino.**

Virgin and Child with Saints by Simone Martini.

The Madonna del Latte

In the " Madonna del Latte" Nino Pisano was dominated by a feeling for the delicacy of form and by his basically Gothic nature. This means: curving position of the Virgin, dynamism of form, and a hint of a smile on the Virgin's face. In effect, Nino was influenced more by Giovanni Pisano than by his own father Andrea. The " Madonna del Latte, " Nino's masterpiece, was executed during the first half of the 14th century.for the Church of Santa Maria della Spina. Its refined elegance is typical of the balanced moderation of the Tuscan, and in particular, Pisan sculptural styles. The serene and almost cheerful expression on the Virgin's face and the highly spiritual feeling are revealed through a balance of lines repeated almost infinitely in the extremely sensitive work of Nino Pisano, Pisa's most delicate and human artist.

St. Paul

The real name of Masaccio, the young painter who worked in Pisa in 1426, was Tommaso di Messer Guidi. The altarpiece which he painted for the Church of the Carmine in Pisa was dismembered and ended up in five different museums: the National Gallery of London, the Lanckoronsky Collection in Vienna, the Friedrich Museum in Berlin, the National Museum of Naples, and the National Museum of Pisa. The St. Paul which remained in Pisa is possibly the most expressive figure in the whole work. Masaccio's fertile, tempestuous artistic talent reached its fulfillment in this balanced yet forceful figure. Unfortunately, the painter's development goes no further than 1428 when he died at the age of 27.

Masaccio boldly shook off the shackles of the decadent Gothic style, imposing his art with all the ardor of the new artistic wave of which he was the leader. In fact he is considered the greatest artist in the post-Gothic pre-Renaissance transition period. While it would be hard to pick out artists who specifically influenced him, we may mention the Florentine architect Filippo Brunelleschi whose way of using perspective reappears in several painters' works. The St. Paul in the National Museum through his powerful, monumental appearance, expresses an inner charge of deep humanity which transcends the typical symbolism and idealization of the late Gothic style. The figure of St. Paul thus becomes an early representative of the realistic approach, almost revolutionary in the way Masaccio treats his subject as a man of the people and, as such, authentic and real, St. Paul in Masaccio's eyes is, in the first place a man of his times and secondly a glorious saint It is by being faithful to his own times that man can reveal the importance of his earthly journey in the reality of a dawning new age.

Above, from the left: *Virgin and Child by Gentile da Fabriano* and *St. Sebastian and St. Rocco by Domenico Ghirlandaio.*

Battle between Pythons and Putti by Spartaco Carlini.

Probably the most talented painter to have come out of Pisa in the last hundred years, Carlini worked in his city during the early 20th century. His personality may be described as modest, simple, serene, and he was fiercely opposed to all kinds of publicity and exterior demonstrations of interest in him or his work, since he looked inward for comfort and inspiration.

THE CHURCH OF
THE SANTO SEPOLCRO

It is believed that this church was built by Diotisalvi sometime during the second half of the 12th century for the Temple Knights. The structure recalls another building in Pisa: the Chapel of Sant' Agatha. As can be easily seen, it differs sharply from the usual Pisan architectural styles.

The church of Santo Sepolcro.
Opposite page: **the sturdy pillars inside the church support the high dome.**

The contours of the church of Santa Maria della Spina seen from the Lungarno; left: *interior of the church, detail.* Opposite page: *the façade.*

SANTA MARIA DELLA SPINA

Originally this tiny church was below the present street level, but then in 1871 owing to constant floods, it was taken apart piece by piece and rebuilt on the new road level.

The side facing the river is the most elaborate. There are thirteen statues depicting Christ and the Twelve Apostles in the niches on the upper section. They have been attributed to Giovanni Pisano. Still higher up in the niches and spires around the top numerous figures of saints and angels enrich the Gothic architecture.

The huge rose window which adorns the façade is a copy of the original now displayed in the National Museum. On the other hand, the marble group representing the Virgin with angels placed lower down in the central area is definitely an authentic piece. In fact, it has been attributed to pupils of Giovanni Pisano.

Preceding page: *the façade of the church of San Paolo a Ripa d'Arno.*
Above: *detail of the decorations over the main door;*
right: *the octagonally shaped chapel of Sant'Agata.*

SAN PAOLO ─ A RIPA D'ARNO

The Church of San Paolo a Ripa d'Arno, erected around 805, is possibly the oldest church in Pisa. It is a splendid example of Pisan Romanesque, outstanding for its great architectural beauty.

Behind the Church of San Paolo stands the tiny Chapel of Sant' Agatha which was built after the Battle of Palermo in 1063. The delightful octagonal-shaped brick building is crowned by a huge spire.

The Medicean lungarni.

THE CITADEL

The Citadel or Shipyard of the Republic is now but a dim recollection of what the real Pisan shipyard was once like. Modern highways, noisy cars, and jets darting about are not enough to erase the memory of the skillful, diligent workers who, decade after decade throughout the Middle Ages, valiantly toiled to keep the city's fleet in good repair. It is very possible that by the beginning of the 13th century the shipyard was already in operation. Sturdy towers and walls were put up to defend this valuable place where brave sea captains had their ships repaired before setting sail eastwards along the fabulous Oriental trade routes. Then in 1406, the first time Florence conquered the city, the Florentines fortified the shipyard even better so that it would be able to withstand any attack. Finally hundreds of years later the Citadel was brutally destroyed in 1943.

The Citadel dominated by the thirteenth century Guelf Tower; below: **the old shipyard where the galleys of the Pisan navy were repaired (XIII century).**

The apse of the basilica of San Pietro a Grado;
left: *a detail of the basilica's interior.*
Opposite page: *the interior withe ciborium and the ruins of the early Christian temple.*

THE BASILICA OF SAN PIETRO A GRADO

The starkly simple church rises majestic and solemn in the silence of the Pisan countryside.

It is a magnificent example of a Romanesque basilica without a façade and a unique one of a church with four apses. The basilica was highly venerated during the Middle Ages, since legend would have it that in the year 44 A. D. St. Peter stopped off here on his way from Antioch to Rome.

The Charterhouse of Pisa; left: *the church façade.*

THE CHARTERHOUSE OF PISA

This Charterhouse is the second largest in Italy after Pavia. It was founded in 1366, whereas the church on the inside was begun in 1374 and finished at the end of the century. The huge flight of stairs on the outside was reconstructed in the 15th century and then retouched again in 1718. Set amidst ancient trees, the Charterhouse of Pisa rises out of the quiet of the Pisan countryside, as if it alone were the solemn symbol of an epoch and a civilization.

THE ESTATE OF SAN ROSSORE

San Rossore is a huge forest filled with Mediterranean pines and other typically Mediterranean vegetation. In 1535 Alessandro dei Medici came into the property, formerly in the hands of the priests of the Pisa Cathedral. In 1789 the Lorraine Grand Duke, Pietro Leopoldo, who was at the time ruler of Tuscany, permanently took possession of San Rossore. The estate in now a favorite retreat for the Republic of Italy's presidents.

A view of the lush vegetation in the San Rossore forest.

FOLKLORE

A city as old and as historic as Pisa could not be without its own folklore which takes us back to old traditions and exciting events. Pisan folklore is particularly rich in this field, but the city's favorites are undoubtedly: the candlelight ceremony (la Luminaria), the Bridge Game (il Gioco del Ponte), the St. Ranieri Boat Race, and the Boat Race of the Four Maritime Republics.

La Luminaria

Since the first half of the 14th century, it has been a Pisan custom to adorn the city's windows with lights on June 16; the eve of the feast-day of St. Ranieri, the Patron Saint of Pisa. On the evening of June 16 following those typical lovely Pisan springtime days, all the buildings along the river are aglow with flickering lights reflected in the Arno. Their glitter gets mixed up with the thousands and thousands of " lampanini " which are set on the water, giving the city a truly fairytale look.

The Gioco del Ponte

This sham fight was originally called the Gioco del Mazzascudo and used to be held in Piazza dei Cavalieri. It mainly served to keep the Pisan youths in fine training in the arts of war. Later the game was played on the " Ponte di Mezzo, " that is, the central bridge of the city. Since the Arno divides Pisa into two parts, the southern side was baptized " Mezzogiorno, " and the northern side " Tramontana. " Knights and soldiers dressed in armor and carrying special shields called " targoni " fight to capture the bridge. Glory and honor go to the winners, austerity ("complete darkness") awaits the losers.

The St. Ranieri Boat Race

The race is held on June 17, the feast-day of St. Ranieri, with the various neighborhoods of the city as contestants After having sailed approximately two thousand meters (a bit more than a mile), to the finish line, a member of the crew of each boat must climb a pole and take down a flag. The winners get a cup, the losers a pair of ducks.

The Regatta Of The Four Maritime Republics

This historic regatta was first raced in 1956 and the idea, which originated in Pisa, has, turned out to be a big national and international success. Once every four years, Pisa, Amalfi, Genoa, and Venice play host to the boat race which is an attempt to perpetuate the memory and splendor of the old maritime republics. Before the race there is a fantastic parade in historic dress to recapture the antique grandeur which, although filtered by time, is still alive and felt. On the figurehead of each boat is the symbol of its republic: for Pisa the eagle, for Amalfi the winged horse, for Genoa the winged dragon, and for Venice the lion of St. Mark.

INDEX

Pisa in History	Page	3
Pisa in Art		6

BAPTISTRY — 40
- *Interior* — 42
- *Pulpit* — 44
- *Pulpit, The Nude Hercules* — 46

CAMPANO TOWER — 85

CAMPOSANTO MONUMENTAL CEMETERY — 55
- *The Bombing* — 56
- *Tabernacle* — 56
- *Chains* — 62
- *Sarcophagi* — 63
- *Frescoes* — 64
- *Removing the Frescoes* — 65

CATHEDRAL — 19
- *Center Door* — 24
- *St. Ranieri's Door* — 27
- *Interior* — 30
- *Pulpit* — 32
- *Panel Painting, the Crucifixion* — 34
- *Panel Painting, The Nativity* — 34
- *Caryatids* — 35
- *Galileo's Lamp* — 36
- *Mosaics* — 37
- *Virgin and Child* — 38
- *St. Agnes* — 38
- *Monument to Henry VII of Luxembourg* — 39
- *St. Ranieri's Urn* — 39

CHARTERHOUSE OF PISA — 106

CHURCHES :
- ABBEY OF SAN ZENO — 76
- BASILICA OF SAN PIETRO A GRADO — 104
- SAN FRANCESCO — 81
- SAN FREDIANO — 83
- SAN PAOLO A RIPA D'ARNO — 101
- SAN SISTO — 82
- SANTA CATERINA — 74
- SANTA MARIA DELLA SPINA — 98
- SANTO SEPOLCRO — 96
- SANTO STEFANO DEI CAVALIERI — 80

CITADEL — Page 103
Etruscan Lion — 53

FOLKLORE — 108
- *The Gioco del Ponte* — 26
- *La Luminaria* — 26
- *Regatta of the Four Maritime Republics* — 26
- *The St. Ranieri Boat Race* — 26

GALILEO GALILEI — 70

Jewish Cemetery and Synagogue — 53

LEANING TOWER — 8

THE MUSEO DELL'OPERA DEL DUOMO — 47
- *Griffon and Basin, Islamic Bronzes* — 48
- *Headless Female Statues* — 49
- *Wooden Christ* — 50
- *Virgin of the Smile* — 51
- *Ivory Madonna* — 52

THE MUSEUM OF THE SINOPIAS — 66
- *Upper floor* — 68
- *Groundfloor* — 69

THE SAN MATTEO NATIONAL MUSEUM — 87
- *Battle of the Pythons and Putti by Spartaco Carlini* — 95
- *Crucifix by Giunta Pisano* — 90
- *Crucifix by Berlinghieri* — 90
- *"Madonna del Latte"* — 92
- *St. Paul* — 94

PALACES:
- AGOSTINI — 86
- ALLA GIORNATA — 85
- GAMBACORTI — 24
- TOSCANELLI — 86

PIAZZAS :
- DEI CAVALIERI — 77
- DELLA BERLINA — 21

SAN ROSSORE ESTATE — 107

UNIVERSITY OF PISA — 84

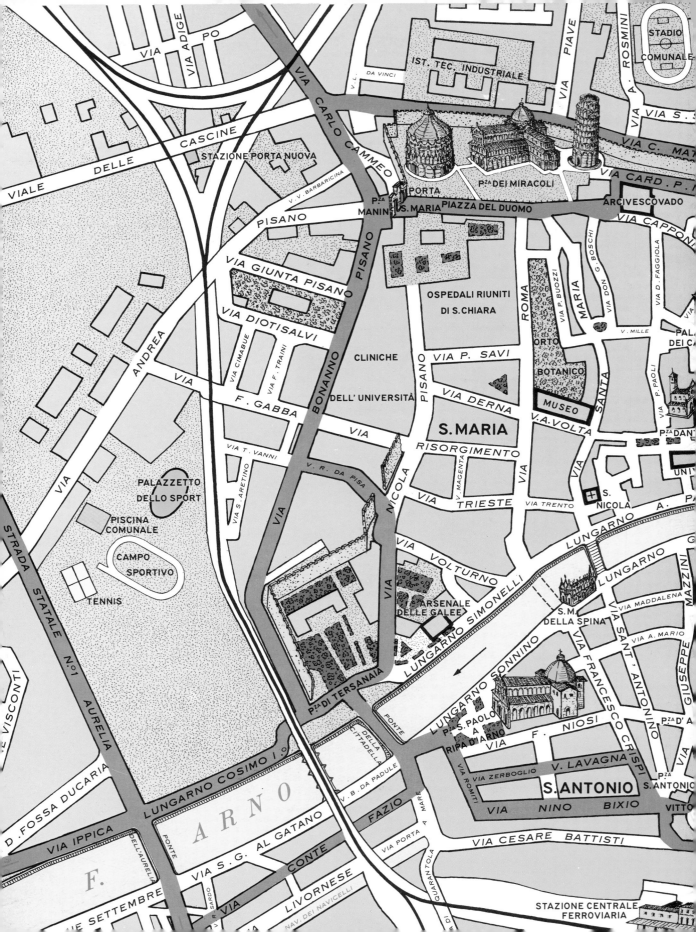

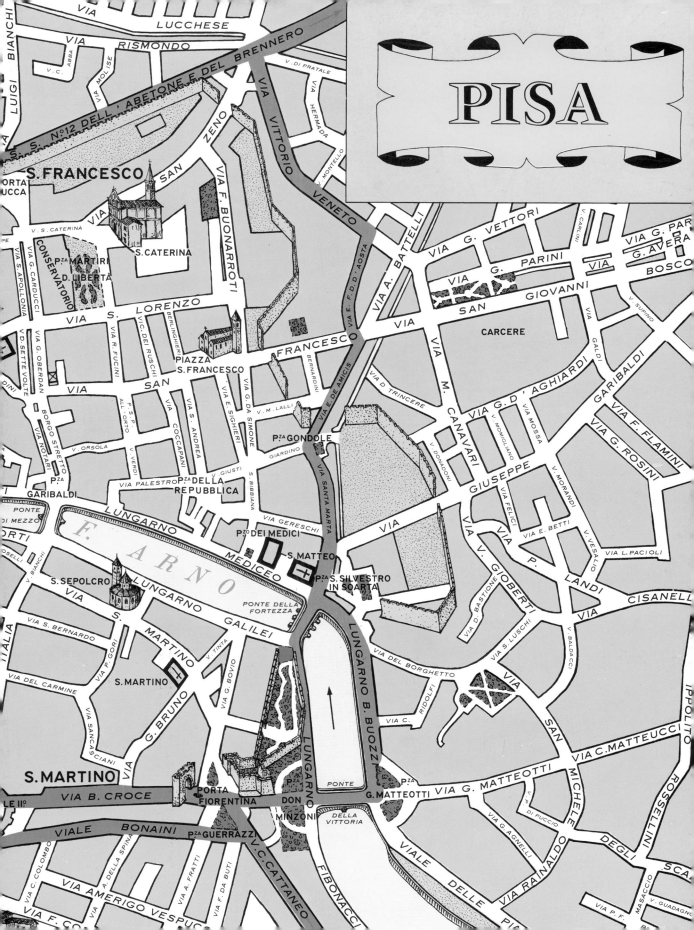